PLANT-POWERED
SWEETS & TREATS

35 Healthy
DESSERTS
to Rejuvenate
Your Whole Body

Dr. Amanda Levitt

ALTERNATIVE
DAILY

CONTENTS

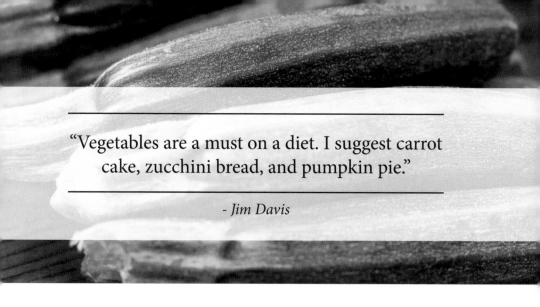

WHOLE FOODS MOSTLY PLANT-BASED DESSERTS

As a naturopathic doctor and mom of three, I'm naturally passionate about nutrition. We cook the majority of our meals at home and do our best to follow a "mostly" whole food, plant-based diet. So, you may be surprised to learn that our family loves dessert!

But desserts don't need to be high in fat or packed with refined sugar to be delicious. You can make healthier homemade desserts that actually add nutrients to your diet.

I'd like to share my collection of whole food, mostly plant-based dessert recipes, which I hope you will enjoy. While desserts are not calorie-free, they can be wholesome and include real food and nutrient dense ingredients that can be enjoyed in moderation.

The recipes I have compiled highlight fruits, vegetables, nuts, seeds, and of course, flavonoid-rich chocolate.

All recipes are gluten-free, and most are dairy-free, vegan, and even free of refined sugars. Most can be modified with substitutions to accommodate dietary restrictions, food allergies or sensitivities.

HELPFUL HINTS FOR SUBSTITUTIONS

- Egg substitute in baked goods: 2 eggs = 2 tablespoons of ground flax seeds added to 6 tablespoons of boiling water. Allow the mixture to sit for 15 minutes and then whisk with a fork.

- Dairy milk substitute: Use the same amount of any unsweetened plant-based milk such as almond, soy, coconut, rice, oat, hemp, pea or cashew milk.

- For tree nut or peanut allergies: Substitute sunflower seeds or pumpkin seeds. For peanut butter, substitute SunButter.

- Gluten-Free Flour substitute: Gluten-free baking flours can be bought in a grocery or health food store. I like Bob's Red Mill Blend, or simply make your own.

This all-purpose gluten-free flour blend and be used for all your gluten-free baking.

- ½ cup rice flour

- ¼ cup tapioca starch/flour

- ¼ cup cornstarch or potato starch

- If you don't have gluten free flour and have no need to restrict gluten in your diet, you can substitute whole wheat pastry flour.

Get creative and make these recipes your own!

WHAT DOES PLANT-BASED MEAN? AND HOW DOES IT RELATE TO DESSERT?

"If it came from a plant, eat it;
if it was made IN a plant, don't. "

- Michael Pollan

A plant-based diet is centered on whole, unrefined, or minimally refined plants. It is a diet based on fruits, vegetables, tubers (root vegetables), nuts and seeds, whole grains, and legumes. It minimizes or excludes animal proteins (including chicken, turkey, pork, beef, lamb, and fish), dairy products, and eggs, as well as highly refined foods like bleached, refined flour and refined sugar.

I like the term "mostly" plant-based, as it is less restrictive. It leaves some wiggle room for other foods to be used in moderation. For those that feel better with higher protein, add small amounts of cold water fish, free range poultry, or grass-fed meat, while keeping vegetables, whole grains, and other plant based foods as key components in your diet.

Plant foods are packed with phytonutrients including vitamins, minerals, fiber, antioxidants, polyphenols, anti-inflammatory agents, and anti-cancer compounds.

Numerous studies have found a strong correlation between a plant-based diet and longevity, immunity, improved mental health, and virtually every health measure you can think of. The science is clear: a plant-based diet is important for the prevention of chronic diseases like heart disease, type 2 diabetes, cancer, and Alzheimer's, to name just a few.

The American Academy of Nutrition and Dietetics and the American Diabetes Association both recommend a plant-based diet as being the most effective nutritional approach when it comes to managing blood glucose levels and preventing metabolic conditions such as diabetes. A Lyon Diet Heart Study, for example, found that the Mediterranean diet, which relies heavily on plant based foods, reduced the incidence of cardiovascular disease by 70 percent compared to the typical American diet.

The American Cancer Society also published a recommendation urging cancer survivors to eat a plant-based diet. The National Cancer Institute offered similar advice. The NCI contends that between 30 and 50 percent of cancers are diet-related and that eating a variety of fresh fruits, vegetables, whole grains, and fiber-rich foods is the best way to ward off cancer.

I hope that this cookbook will encourage you to take one more step down the dietary path towards health. While you are enjoying these plant-powered desserts, you can savor the fact that you are improving your health, preventing disease, and having a lower impact on our planet...and enjoying some new and delicious recipes at the same time!

IS CHOCOLATE A HEALTH FOOD?

"All you need is love. But a little chocolate now and then doesn't hurt!"

- Charles M. Schultz

Do you love chocolate? I do!

My husband and I recently traveled to Belize where we had the honor of visiting a chocolate plantation in order to participate in the ancient Mayan ritual of making chocolate from cocoa beans. Chocolate is produced from the beans of the cacao tree (Theobroma cacao).

Not only is chocolate a decadent treat that many of us crave, but you may be surprised to hear that high-quality chocolate can actually be good for you. Chocolate contains powerful plant chemicals called flavonols that a growing body of research supports the protective effects of this superfood.

TOP HEALTH BENEFITS OF CHOCOLATE

- Nutrient Dense Superfood: Dark chocolate is an excellent source of soluble fiber, phytonutrients, and essential minerals. In particular, it's an excellent source of iron, manganese, copper, and magnesium, as well as potassium, selenium, and zinc.

- Antioxidant Power! Cocoa beans are an antioxidant powerhouse that protects against the oxidation of cholesterol and prevents damage to the lining of arteries.

- Reduce Heart Disease: Studies have found that flavanols in dark chocolate stimulate the production of nitric oxide in the bloodstream, which improves blood flow and optimizes blood pressure. In fact, frequent chocolate consumption is associated with a lower risk of heart disease and stroke.

- Improve Cognitive Function: Cocoa contains compounds like caffeine and theobromine, which have been shown to improve several aspects of cognitive function.

- Stress Reduction: Chocolate can blunt the stress response and reduce the negative effects of stress on the body. People who consume small amounts of dark chocolate regularly tend to have lower levels of the stress hormone cortisol.

All chocolate is NOT created equal. I'm not talking about the low-quality chocolate brands that most people are familiar with, which usually contain loads of sugar, calories, and high fructose corn syrup. In fact, most commercial candy bars (like Snickers or Milky Way) are not even allowed to be marketed as chocolate bars, due to their low chocolate content. They have to be labeled "candy bars."

To reap the health benefits of chocolate:

- Choose higher-quality dark chocolate, which contains at least 70 percent cocoa.
- One ounce per day (about two small squares) delivers the optimum benefits. Even high-quality dark chocolate contains calories and fat, so it's important to remember that when it comes to chocolate, there is a sweet spot, which is to say that the biggest benefits come from enjoying it in moderation.
- Many of these recipes combine chocolate with fruit, nuts, and seeds to deliciously boost fiber and antioxidant power.

HOMEMADE VERSUS STORE-BOUGHT DESSERTS

"You are what you eat, so don't be
fast, cheap, easy, or fake."

-Unknown

Desserts are a treat, but that doesn't mean that they should be filled with chemicals and other additives that are harmful to your health. If you read the label on many grocery store baked goods, you may be rightfully dismayed to find unrecognizable ingredients that are not food. Mono and diglycerides, high fructose corn syrup, FD&C Yellow #5, sodium benzoate, partially hydrogenated oils...these are ingredients that have no place on your plate... in a dessert or a healthy diet.

When you prepare food at home, you have control over what you are feeding yourself and your family. I would much prefer to consume and serve desserts with high-quality, real food ingredients (that means no artificial additives that you need a chemistry degree to decipher).

"Don't eat anything your great-grandmother wouldn't recognize as food."

- Michael Pollan

REFINED VERSUS UNREFINED, NATURAL SWEETENERS:

Sugar in all forms is a simple carbohydrate that your body converts into glucose to use for energy. But, not all sugar is created equal. The type of sugar that you consume has different effects on your body and overall health.

Refined sugar refers to sugar processed from sugarcane or sugar beets.
Your body breaks down refined sugar rapidly, causing blood sugar and insulin levels to spike and then drop below baseline, causing blood sugar dysregulation. Not only does refined sugar cause a roller coaster of blood sugar levels because it has been stripped of fiber and nutrients, but it is also a source of empty calories and does not make you feel full. This, unfortunately, leads to overeating and weight gain.

How does this affect health?

High refined sugar intake is associated with obesity, cancer, metabolic syndrome, diabetes, and heart disease.

NATURAL SWEETENERS:

Better choices for sweeteners include unrefined, less refined or natural sugars like honey, maple syrup, coconut sugar, brown rice syrup, molasses, applesauce, bananas, and dates. These sweeteners still have calories, but they are less refined, so they still contain vitamins, minerals, and other nutrients. Most importantly, they have a lower glycemic index, which means less of a roller coaster effect on your blood sugar. Use natural sweeteners in moderation instead of refined sugars.

WHAT ABOUT ARTIFICIAL SWEETENERS?

The FDA has approved five non-caloric artificial sweeteners (saccharin, acesulfame, aspartame, neotame, and sucralose) for human consumption marketed under the trade names Sweet and Low, Sugar Twin, Sweet One, Nutrasweet, Equal, and Splenda to name a few. These synthetic chemicals do not raise blood glucose levels directly the way sugars do, but numerous studies have linked them to a wide range of serious medical problems including heart disease, strokes, migraines, diabetes, obesity, and inflammatory disorders. I caution my patients against using artificial sweeteners. The risks highly outweigh any benefit.

ARE STEVIA OR ALCOHOL SUGARS A BETTER CHOICE?

- Stevia is a plant-derived sweetener extracted from the leaves of the *Stevia rebaudiana* (sweetleaf) plant. Stevia-sweetened products contain a compound called Rebaudioside A with some proportion of stevioside, which tastes 100 to 300 times sweeter than table sugar. It is marketed under the trade names of Truvia, Purevia, and Sweetleaf, and is also available as a liquid or powdered extract for cooking. It is surprisingly sweet, and like the synthetic chemicals above, it has minimal impact on blood sugar levels.

   Stevia extracts are a processed sweetener, but safe to use in moderate amounts. I consider stevia to be a better choice than artificial sweeteners. Alternatively, you can also grow stevia plants at home and use the leaves as a natural sweetener. Be aware that stevia leaves or less purified stevia products, like powdered leaves or whole plant extracts have a slightly bitter or licorice aftertaste.

- Erythritol, sorbitol, xylitol, and maltitol are alcohol sugars that have fewer calories and less negative blood sugar or insulin effects than refined sugar. They have a similar structure to sugar, so they stimulate sweet receptors on the tongue. Alcohol sugars like xylitol and erythritol have beneficial effects on oral health and the prevention of cavities.

  Since alcohol sugars are not fully digested, gut bacteria feeding on these alcohol sugars release methane and hydrogen gas as a byproduct, which can cause digestive distress like gas, bloating, cramping and unwanted laxative effects if eaten in large amounts. In small amounts, however, they are generally well tolerated. But for those with irritable bowel syndrome or sensitivity to FODMAPs, alcohol sugars may not be your best choice of sweeteners.

  Of the alcohol sugars, erythritol and xylitol tend to cause the least amount of digestive symptoms. Xylitol is toxic for dogs, so keep out of reach of your canine companions.

  Bottom line: I recommend being aware of the gastrointestinal side effects of alcohol type sweeteners and using them sparingly.

The very best sweetener is fruit, packed with fiber to balance blood sugar, feed beneficial gut bacteria, and encourage satiety. Fruit also contains antioxidants to reduce cancer, inflammatory diseases, and heart disease risk, as well as a wide array of vitamins and minerals.

"Everything in moderation, including moderation."

- Oscar Wilde

POWER
PACKED
FUDGE

. . . .

[GF, DF, V]

Healthy fudge! This no-cook recipe yields a delicious, but nutritious fudge that can fool even the most dedicated chocoholics. The nut butters add protein and the brown rice syrup is a great non-refined sweetener. You can feel good sharing this treat with your family and friends. It is surprisingly simple to make, yet it looks fancy enough to bring to an office or holiday party. It also makes for a yummy but healthy and energy-boosting snack you can take on the go!

1 cup of almond, peanut, or cashew butter

½ to ¾ cup of brown rice syrup or honey

1 teaspoon vanilla extract

½ cup of carob or cocoa powder

Shredded coconut, chopped nuts, dried cranberries, blueberries, or raisins (optional)

1   Combine nut butter, brown rice syrup, and vanilla into a smooth paste.

2   With clean hands, knead in the carob or cocoa powder until the mixture becomes a shiny dough.

3   Press the mixture into a pan until it is about a ½-inch thick and then cut into desired shapes (have fun with small cookie cutters, or roll into balls, cut into squares, etc.)

4   Chopped nuts, coconut, or dried fruit can be added to the mixture before shaping, or simply sprinkle on top if desired.

CHOCOLATE
BARK

· ·

[GF, DF, V]

The possibilities are endless. Mix and match your favorite fruits, nuts, or seeds. Raw nuts are delicious, but roasting really brings out the flavor.

Good quality dark chocolate (Trader Joe's has a 72% Dark Cocoa Pound Plus bar that works well)

MIX INS:

Roasted or raw walnuts, pecans, pumpkin seeds, cashews

Shredded coconut

Dried cranberries or cherries

Freeze dried raspberries or strawberries

1   Prepare a pan or plate by covering with parchment paper.

2   Carefully set up a double boiler by placing a bowl over a pot of boiling water. Be sure the inside of the bowl and the spoon stay dry, as introducing water will produce a grainy texture in the chocolate.

3   Break the chocolate into small pieces and add to double boiler bowl and stir until ⅔ of the chocolate is melted. Remove carefully from heat and stir until fully melted.

4   Pour chocolate onto parchment paper covered pan or plate.

5   Sprinkle with desired toppings.

6   Allow to set in the refrigerator.

7   Once hardened, break into pieces and enjoy!

FRUIT
"NACHOS"

· ·

[GF, DF, V]

This colorful and nutritious take on nachos is a fun and festive way to serve fruit. Get creative and substitute seasonal fruit and toppings to taste.

4 pears or apples,
cored and thinly
sliced

½ teaspoon cinnamon

1/2 mango,
finely chopped

1/4 cup chopped
strawberries

2 Tablespoons
shaved coconut

1/4 cup toasted
sliced almonds

2 Tbsp melted
chocolate or
2 tablespoons of mini
chocolate chips

1 cup vanilla Greek
yogurt or coconut
yogurt for vegan-
optional

1   Arrange pear or apple slices on a platter.

2   Sprinkle with cinnamon.

3   Sprinkle mango, strawberries, coconut and almonds over top.

4   Drizzle evenly with melted chocolate or sprinkle with mini chips.

5   Drizzle with vanilla Greek yogurt or use as dipping sauce (optional).

PEANUT BUTTER **COOKIE**

....

Almost guilt-free, these simple sweet and nutty flourless high protein cookies have only 4 ingredients.

1 cup of all natural creamy peanut butter or almond butter- stir well if oil separates

5 Tablespoons 100% maple syrup

1 teaspoon white sesame seeds

Salt to taste (important if using unsalted peanut butter)

1 Preheat the oven to 350°F.

2 Line a baking sheet with parchment paper.

3 In a food processor, add the peanut butter, maple syrup, and ½ tsp salt Process on high until cookie dough thickens and forms a solid mass, about 1 to 2 minutes.

4 Roll the cookie dough into 10-12 even balls and transfer to the lined baking sheet.

5 Use the back of a fork to press a criss-cross pattern into each cookie, flattening each ball into a circle about ½ inch thick.

6 Sprinkle with sesame seeds.

7 Bake cookies until they brown slightly, about 10 to 12 minutes. Do not overcook. Allow to cool completely before removing from the lined baking sheet, as these flourless cookies will be crumbly when hot!

CHOCOLATE CHIP PEANUT BUTTER COCONUT FLOUR COOKIES

If you like a low-carb, soft and chewy cookie with peanut butter and chocolate, you are in luck!

[GF, DF, V]

½ cup nut butter (peanut, almond, cashew, or sunbutter)

2 tablespoons coconut oil

½ cup coconut sugar or light brown sugar

2 eggs (or vegan egg replacement: 2 Tablespoons of ground flax meal mixed with 5 tablespoons of water, let sit for 5 minutes and use as an egg substitute)

1½ teaspoons vanilla extract

½ teaspoon baking soda

¼ teaspoon ground cinnamon

¼ teaspoon salt

½ cup coconut flour

½ cup chocolate chips (use dairy-free for vegan)

1 Preheat oven to 350°F and line a baking sheet with parchment paper.

2 In a food processor, combine nut butter, coconut oil and coconut sugar until smooth. Add eggs (or an egg substitute) and vanilla and blend until smooth.

3 Add baking soda, cinnamon, salt, and coconut flour. Process until smooth dough forms. With a spatula, fold in chocolate chips.

4 To form cookies, use a heaping tablespoon of dough for each cookie dropped onto the prepared baking sheet and gently flatten each cookie with fingers or fork.

5 Bake for 6-7 minutes, or until cookies are golden brown on the edges, but still quite soft. Cool on baking tray for 3 minutes and then transfer to wire rack to finish cooling.

FROZEN
CHOCOLATE
COVERED
BANANAS

· ·

[GF, DF, V]

*My kids go nuts for these
chocolate covered bananas
rolled in peanuts.*

8 Bananas, peeled and cut in half

32 ounces of good quality chocolate or chocolate chips

2-3 tablespoons coconut oil

Crushed nuts

Coconut flakes

Popsicle sticks

1 Prepare a tray or plate by covering with parchment paper.

2 Insert popsicle sticks into the cut end of bananas, pushing the stick halfway in and leaving half of the stick as a handle.

3 Freeze bananas on tray for 1 hour prior to dipping to avoid breaking.

4 Melt chocolate and coconut oil in a double boiler, be careful not to introduce any water into the bowl.

5 Remove chocolate from heat, stir.

6 Carefully dip banana into chocolate to cover.

7 Roll banana in desired toppings, or place on prepared tray and sprinkle with toppings.

8 Return bananas to the freezer until fully frozen. Store frozen treats in an airtight container.

PECAN DATE
ROLLS

. . . .

[GF, DF, V]

Pecans and dates are a delicious combination, it's like pecan pie on the go!

1 cup, packed, soft pitted dates

1 cup pecans

1/2 tsp sea salt

1/2 tsp pure vanilla extract

1   Place dates, pecans, sea salt, and vanilla extract into food processor.

2   Pulse and mix until it forms a dough.

3   Using a spatula, remove the dough and roll into balls.

4   Press pecan half or pieces into the top if desired.

5   Store in refrigerator.

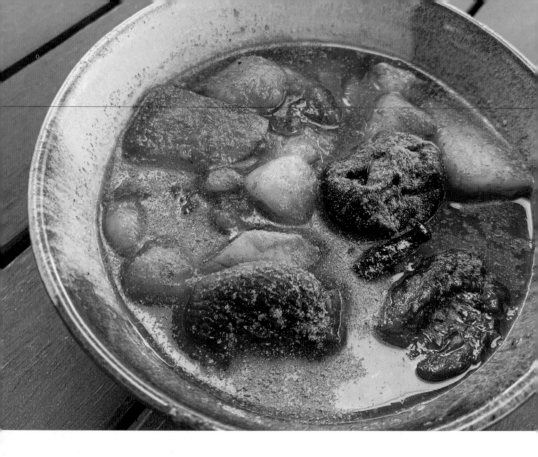

FRUIT
COMPOTE

. . . .

[GF, DF, V]

A compote is a dessert originating from medieval Europe. It is traditionally made with fresh or dried fruit simmered in a syrup flavored with spices. Top this sweet, warming dessert with Cashew Cream.

½ cup dried apricots

1 apple, thinly sliced

¼ cup prunes, pitted

1 pear, sliced

1 cinnamon stick

⅛ teaspoon nutmeg

½ teaspoon vanilla extract

1 cup apple juice

1   Place all ingredients in a medium-sized pot and bring to a boil.

2   Cover and lower heat to simmer, until all fruit is soft, approximately 20-30 minutes.

3   Remove cinnamon stick.

4   Divide compote into bowls and top with Cashew Cream.

CASHEW
CREAM

. . . .

[GF, DF, V]

This creamy nut blend is a rich, delicious, non-dairy topping to substitute for whipped cream or frosting. Seriously, it is surprisingly scrumptious!

½ cup raw, unsalted cashews

3 tablespoons of 100% maple syrup

2 teaspoons vanilla extract

Water

1 Using a food processor or grinder, grind nuts to a fine meal.

2 Add ground cashews, maple syrup, and vanilla into a blender.

3 With blender running, slowly add water until you achieve desired creamy consistency.

4 Add a dollop to fresh berries or as a topping for compote.

LEMON
CUSTARD

· ·

[GF, DF, V]

This light, lemony custard is a refreshing dessert. Lovely topped with sliced strawberries.

1 cup plain rice milk

2 tablespoon
agar flakes

¾ cup brown
rice syrup

2 tablespoons sucanat
or raw sugar

⅛ teaspoon turmeric

Pinch of sea salt

2 Tablespoons
arrowroot

¼ cup water

½ cup fresh squeezed
lemon juice

½ cup sliced
strawberries to
garnish

1 Mix rice milk, agar, brown rice syrup, sucanat, turmeric and salt in a medium pot.

2 Bring to a boil, whisking until agar has dissolved, about 5 minutes.

3 Strain through a sieve to remove any undissolved agar chunks, and return to the pot to simmer on low.

4 In a separate bowl, mix arrowroot, water, and vanilla together. Add to simmering mixture and cook until thickened and translucent, about 2-3 minutes.

5 Remove from heat and add lemon juice. Mix well.

6 Pour into individual ramekins and chill in refrigerator until firm. Garnish with strawberry slices.

TOFU
CHEESECAKE

· ·

[GF, DF, V]

If you love cheesecake but could do without the lactose, fat, and calories, try this healthier version! Be sure to choose organic, non-gmo silken tofu.

CRUST:

1¼ cup gluten free rolled oats

⅓ cup ground hazelnuts

½ cup gluten-free flour

¼ cup olive oil

2 tablespoons maple syrup

1-2 tablespoons water

FILLING:

2 packages of silken tofu (10-ounces)

½ teaspoon sea salt

3 tablespoon freshly squeezed lemon juice

7 tablespoons 100% maple syrup

3 tablespoons tahini

2 teaspoons vanilla extract

¼ teaspoon almond extract

½ teaspoon rice vinegar

1 tablespoon of kudzu dissolved in ¼ cup of cold water

TOPPING:

**½ cup of
raspberry jam**

**2 tablespoons of
kudzu or arrowroot
dissolved in ½ cup of
cold water**

CRUST:

1. Preheat oven to 350°F.

2. Grind oats and nuts in a food processor.

3. In a mixing bowl, combine oat/nut mixture and flour.

4. In a separate bowl, mix oil and maple syrup together.

5. Combine wet and dry ingredients, adding 1-2 tablespoons of water if needed to form the dough.

6. Press the mixture into lightly oiled 9-inch pie pan.

7. Bake for 10-12 minutes. Remove from oven and set aside. Lower oven heat to 300°F for baking cheesecake.

FILLING:

1 Combine tofu, salt, lemon juice, maple syrup, tahini, vanilla, almond extract, vinegar, and dissolved kudzu in a blender or food processor. Blend until smooth.

2 Pour filling into pre-baked pie crust and bake for 25 minutes. Turn off oven and let pie rest in hot oven turned off for another 20 minutes.

3 Set aside to cool covered in refrigerator.

TOPPING:

1 Combine jam and dissolved kudzu in a pot.

2 Stir constantly with a whisk over medium heat until thick and translucent.

3 Let topping cool slightly before pouring over cheesecake.

SWEET CORN MUFFINS WITH **WINTER SQUASH**

These muffins are dense, but sweet and satisfying. Great use for leftover butternut squash, pumpkin, or sweet potato.

. . . .

[GF, DF, V]

1½ cup cornmeal

1½ cup gluten free flour

1 tablespoon baking powder

¼ teaspoon sea salt

⅛ tsp cinnamon

2 cups of sweet potato or butternut squash puree

⅓ cup olive oil

½ cup 100% maple syrup

½ cup water

¼ cup raw pumpkin seeds

1   Preheat oven to 375°F.

2   Lightly oil muffin pan.

3   Mix cornmeal, flour, baking powder, salt, and cinnamon in a bowl.

4   In a separate bowl, whisk together squash puree, oil, syrup, and water until smooth.

5   Combine wet and dry ingredients with a minimum of strokes.

6   Spoon into muffin cups and top each with pumpkin seeds.

7   Bake 20-25 minutes until muffin tops are slightly brown and cracked.

BAKED
APPLE
CASSEROLE

....

[GF, DF, V]

Who doesn't love the sweet
smell of baked apples?
This wholesome dessert is
warming and satisfying.

5 apples, peeled and sliced into chunks

1½ teaspoons cinnamon

3-4 dates, chopped

¼ cup nuts (diced walnuts and pecans work well)

2 tablespoons of coconut oil or butter

1 Preheat the oven to 350°F.

2 Put the apples in a small to medium-sized baking dish.

3 Melt coconut oil or butter and pour over apples.

4 Sprinkle with cinnamon, dates, and nuts.

5 Toss well to coat.

6 Bake in the preheated oven until the apples are soft, about 20-30 minutes. Stir once during the baking time.

CHOCOLATE CHIA **PUDDING** WITH FRESH BERRIES

This classic chia pudding looks (and tastes) impressive garnished with fresh berries and cacao nibs!

. . . .

[GF, DF, V]

2 cups unsweetened nut milk (almond, cashew, etc)

½ cup chia seeds

⅓ cup 100% cocoa/ cacao powder

⅓ cup 100% maple syrup

2 teaspoons vanilla extract

Pinch of sea salt

Berries, banana slices, cacao nibs to garnish (optional)

1 In a medium-sized mixing bowl, combine the nut milk, chia seeds, cocoa powder, maple syrup, vanilla, and salt, whisk well until fully blended, about 2 minutes.

2 Cover and place in the fridge to chill.

3 Stir well after 30 minutes, cover again and continue to chill.

4 Pudding should be thickened and ready to serve within 4 hours, and will be at its thickest after 8-10 hours.

5 Garnish with berries or banana slices and cacao nibs if desired.

MEXICAN CHOCOLATE SAUCE WITH **PINEAPPLE**

[GF, DF, V]

Mexican chocolate with chili powder is a favorite in our household. We love this spicy and sweet sauce served with tangy, fresh pineapple!

¾ cup almond milk

¼ cup dried dates, chopped

1 tsp vanilla extract

1 tsp cinnamon

¼ tsp chipotle powder

½ cup cocoa powder (dark, unsweetened)

1 fresh pineapple, peeled and cut into chunks or spears for dipping

1   In a small pot, combine almond milk, dates, vanilla, cinnamon, and chipotle powder. Bring to a boil, and then promptly reduce heat to a simmer for 2 minutes.

2   Transfer to blender and blend with cocoa powder until smooth.

3   Serve slightly warmed with pineapple chunks or spears.

SEMI SWEET
DARK
CHOCOLATE
PEANUT
BUTTER
CUPS

· ·

[GF, DF, V]

No need to miss out on your favorite treat...try this healthier version of the classic peanut butter cup!

4 oz baker's chocolate or semisweet vegan chocolate chips

½ cup coconut oil

1 teaspoon vanilla extract

Pinch of salt

¼ cup 100% maple syrup

½ cup natural creamy peanut butter (no sugars or oils added)

2 tablespoons chopped peanuts, to garnish

1 Set out a silicone muffin mold or muffin liners in a regular muffin tin.

2 Melt chocolate, coconut oil, vanilla, and maple syrup in a double boiler. Simply using a large bowl placed over a pot of gently boiling water is fine. Avoid letting any water contact the chocolate.

3 Once melted, remove from heat and add a pinch of salt.

4 Spoon 1 tablespoon of the chocolate liquid into each of the 12 muffin cups. Freeze for at least 15 minutes to set.

5 Keep remaining melted chocolate in a warm place on the stove.

6 Once the chocolate has set, spoon 1 scant tablespoon of peanut butter into each chocolate cup.

7 Cover the peanut butter with another tablespoon of the chocolate liquid. Sprinkle with chopped peanuts to garnish.

8 Freeze to set approximately 15 to 20 minutes.

9 Keep frozen until ready to eat.

FRUIT AND CEREAL
ENERGY BAR

. . . .

[GF, DF, V]

Homemade bars are tasty and nutritious. Perfect for on the go snack or breakfast. Add your favorite dried fruits, nuts, and cereal to make these easy, no-bake bars.

2 tablespoon olive oil

1½ cup dried fruits (fig, dates, apricots, raisins, dried cranberries, or cherries)

2-3 tablespoons honey or maple syrup

Fruit juice or water as needed

2 1/2 cups low sugar granola or other low sugar cereal, choose gluten-free if desired.

½ cup chopped nuts or seeds (pecans, walnuts, almonds, sunflower or pumpkin seeds)

1 Lightly grease an 8-inch square baking pan.

2 In a food processor, add dried fruit, oil, and honey and pulse until sticky.

3 Add juice or water 1 tablespoon at a time to break up the fruit.

4 In a large mixing bowl, combine cereal, nuts and fruit mixture until the cereal is coated.

5 Press the cereal and fruit mixture evenly into the prepared pan and chill to set in refrigerator.

6 Cut into squares for an easy snack on the go.

7 Store in airtight container for up to 4 days.

GRAPEFRUIT
BRULEE

. . . .

[GF, DF, V]

Grapefruit Brulee is typically done with a grapefruit sliced in half, which is lovely, but my favorite method of peeling and cutting the grapefruit into rounds is even lovelier! This is a simple recipe, but our family loves the tangy taste of grapefruit with the little bit of sweet crunch from the melted brown sugar.

2 large grapefruits, peeled and sliced into ½ inch thick rounds

Brown sugar

1   Heat broiler and place rack 4-inches from heat source.

2   Place grapefruit rounds on a baking tray on oven rack.

3   Sprinkle with brown sugar.

4   Broil until brown and bubbling.

TAJIN
FRUIT

. . . .

[GF, DF, V]

Tajin is a tangy Mexican blend of lime, mild chili pepper and salt. If you like the zing of spicy and sour, simply topping your tropical fruit with this powdered blend elevates your fruit plate to a whole new level! So simple, yet so delicious sprinkled on cucumbers and jicama too!

Pineapple, peeled and cut into spears

Papaya, peeled and cut into chunks

Watermelon, cut into spears

Tajin powder (found in the Mexican section of the grocery store)

1   Peel and cut fruit into desired shapes.

2   Arrange on a platter.

3   Sprinkle with Tajin and serve immediately.

FRUIT
SORBET

. . . .

[GF, DF, V]

This refreshing and versatile recipe can be used with any fruit to delight your palate.

1 pound of frozen fruit (I love mango, but strawberries, bananas, peaches or any other favorite fruits work well too)

½ cup of plain yogurt, coconut yogurt, or silken tofu

Sweeten with either honey, maple syrup, or stevia to taste

Fresh, chopped fruit or coconut flakes as optional topping

1   Add fruit, yogurt or tofu, and 2 tablespoons of water in a food processor.

2   Process until just pureed and creamy. Add sweetener of choice to taste. Do not over process.

3   Scrape down sides of the container as needed during processing and add 1-2 tablespoons of water as needed to desired consistency.

4   Serve immediately, or transfer to an airtight container and freeze.

5   Thaw for 15 minutes at room temperature before serving if hard from the freezer.

6   Top with fruit or coconut flakes-optional.

FRUITY
ICE POPS

. . . .

[GF, DF, V]

Popsicles are a hot commodity around the pool during the summer. Our kids and their friends clamor to enjoy our homemade popsicles. All natural, no artificial colors or sweeteners! No plastic tubes of blue, artificially flavored pops served here!

2 cups chopped ripe fruit

2 teaspoons of fresh lemon juice

3 tablespoons honey or maple syrup

1 Puree fruit, honey and lemon juice in a blender or food processor. Add 1 tablespoon of water as needed to keep the mixture blending.

2 Once smooth, pour the mixture into popsicle molds or paper cups with popsicle sticks.

3 Freeze until solid, about 3 hours.

MANGO LIME
POPSICLES

[GF, DF, V]

These tropical popsicles are refreshing and hydrating. The perfect treat for a hot summer day!

2 large mangos, peeled, pitted and sliced or 1½ cup frozen mango (defrost for ease of blending)

1 lime, juice and zest

½ cup coconut water

Sweeten to taste with honey, maple syrup, or stevia

1 In a blender, combine mango, lime juice and zest, and coconut water. Blend until smooth. Add more coconut water if the mixture is too thick.

2 Sweeten to taste with sweetener of choice, being sure to blend well.

3 Pour into popsicle molds and freeze overnight.

BANANA BREAD WITH **FLAX MEAL**

·····················

[GF, DF, V]

This sweet and hearty banana bread is packed with fiber, and is a perfect use for those overripe bananas on your counter!

⅓ cup of olive oil

½ cup of coconut sugar

2 eggs or egg substitute

⅓ cup plain yogurt or non-dairy yogurt

1 cup mashed bananas

½ cup gluten-free rolled oats, ground into flour in a blender

¼ cup flax meal

1 cup gluten-free pastry flour

1 teaspoon baking powder

½ teaspoon baking soda

½ teaspoon salt

½ cup crushed pecans or walnuts

1 Preheat oven to 350°F.

2 Oil a 5 x 9 inch bread pan.

3 In a mixing bowl, combine oil and brown sugar. Add eggs and beat well. Mix in yogurt and bananas.

4 In a blender, pulse oats to ground to a flour.

5 In a large bowl, combine oat flour, flax meal, pastry flour, baking powder, baking soda and salt.

6 Add banana mixture and stir with a minimum of strokes.

7 Pour batter into prepared baking pan and sprinkle with nuts.

8 Bake for 1 hour or until middle is firm and knife slides out clean. If nuts are browning too quickly, cover loosely with foil.

FUDGY
BROWNIES

. . . .

[GF, DF]

These fudgy, honey-sweetened brownies are gooey and decadent!

½ cup coconut oil

3 ounces dark chocolate (6 tablespoons of dark chocolate chips)

⅓ cup gluten free pastry flour

¼ cup cocoa powder

½ tsp salt

2 eggs or egg substitute

⅓ cup honey or maple syrup

1 Preheat the oven to 300ºF and lightly oil an 8 x 8 inch square baking dish with coconut oil.

2 In a small saucepan over low heat, melt the coconut oil and dark chocolate. If using a dark chocolate bar, break into smaller pieces. Stir until completely melted.

3 In a small mixing bowl combine flour, cocoa powder and salt.

4 In a separate mixing bowl, combine the eggs, honey, and melted coconut oil chocolate mixture. Stir with a spatula until combined.

5 Add the flour mixture to the chocolate mixture and stir by hand just until combined. Pour the brownie batter into the pan and bake for 25-27 minutes for fudgier brownies.

6 These brownies become fudgier in texture the longer they sit. (If you can resist!)

BERRY
JAM BARS

. . . .

[GF, DF, V]

These bars were served at my children's preschool once a week and sometimes there were leftovers for parents. So good, I always did a silly jam bar dance! For the vegan version, swap butter for earth balance butter substitute.

¾ cup of butter or Earth Balance

1 cup brown sugar or coconut sugar

1½ cup gluten free pastry flour

1 teaspoon salt

½ teaspoon of baking soda

1 1/2 cup gluten free oat bran

12 ounces 100% fruit strawberry or raspberry preserves (jam)

1 Preheat oven to 400°F and lightly oil a 9 x 13 inch baking pan.

2 Beat together butter and sugar until light and fluffy.

3 Add flour, salt, and baking soda. Mix well.

4 Stir in oat bran to make crumb mixture.

5 Press half of the mixture onto the bottom of the prepared baking pan.

6 Spread preserves (jam) over the layer of crumb mixture.

7 Sprinkle remaining crumb mixture over the jam layer.

8 Bake for 25 minutes. Cool and cut into bars.

ZUCCHINI
BREAD

[GF, DF, V]

This moist, flourless zucchini bread is a great way to sneak vegetables and omega 3 rich walnuts into a tasty dessert.

2 1/2 cups gluten free rolled oats

1 cup mashed banana

1 cup finely grated zucchini, loosely packed

1 teaspoon baking soda

1/2 teaspoon cinnamon

½ teaspoon ground cloves

½ teaspoon ginger

3/4 tsp baking powder

3/4 tsp salt

1 1/2 tsp pure vanilla extract

1/3 cup olive oil OR milk of choice (dairy, almond, soy, rice)

1/2 cup pure maple syrup, or honey

1 1/2 tablespoons vinegar

1/2 cup chocolate chips-optional

¼ cup chopped walnuts

1   Preheat oven to 350 F, and grease a 9×5 loaf pan.

2   Add oats to a blender and blend until a fine powder forms.

3   Add all other ingredients (except optional chips) and blend until smooth.

4   Stir in chips, if using.

5   Pour the batter into the prepared pan, and sprinkle with chopped walnuts.

6   Bake on the middle rack for 35 minutes.

7   Turn the oven off, but DON'T open the oven. Let the bread sit in the closed oven for another 10 minutes to continue to bake. Set a timer.

8   Remove from the oven and let cool completely.

9   Carefully run a knife around the sides to loosen, and then invert onto a plate.

CHOCOLATE
DIPPED
MACAROONS

· ·

[GF, DF, V]

These chocolate dipped macaroons are gluten free, so easy to make, and look impressive!

1¼ cups unsweetened small coconut shreds (larger flakes will not hold together as easily)

¼ cup finely ground, blanched almond flour

3 tablespoons solid coconut oil

¼ cup pure maple syrup

Pinch of sea salt

6-12 ounces dark chocolate

1 tablespoon coconut oil

1 Preheat the oven to 350°F. Line a baking sheet with parchment paper and set aside.

2 Add coconut flakes, almond flour, coconut oil, maple syrup, and a pinch of sea salt into a food processor.

3 Blend until it forms a thick and sticky mixture that holds together, with smaller, but still noticeable coconut pieces. If any maple syrup remains at the bottom of the processor, fold into dough until well mixed.

4 Scoop firmly packed balls of coconut mixture and place onto the prepared baking sheet. Be sure to leave room in between each ball.

5 Bake for 10-15 minutes, until golden around the edges and slightly golden on top. If you like chewy macaroons, do not overcook.

6 Allow to cool on a baking rack for 30 minutes.

7 In a small pot, melt the chocolate with the coconut oil. Stir well and remove from heat.

8 Dip each macaroon until half covered in chocolate and set on parchment paper to harden before serving.

BERRIES AND
CREAM

· ·

[GF, DF, V]

Fresh berries are naturally sweet, and look lovely when served with a dollop of whipped cream. This may seem too simple for a recipe book, but our family and dinner guests always love a colorful bowl of berries with topping for dessert! Another variation is to serve berries with a topping of crushed dark chocolate bar and chopped mint leaves!

For a dairy-free or vegan version, substitute cashew cream. (see page 40)

Fresh raspberries, blueberries, and blackberries

Organic heavy whipping cream

Honey or 100% maple syrup to taste

½ teaspoon vanilla extract

Fresh mint for garnish

1   Right before serving, rinse berries gently and pat dry.

2   Place in small ramekins or wine glass.

3   In a mixing bowl, blend cream and vanilla with mixer until whipped cream forms. Add sweetener to taste.

4   Add a dollop of whipped cream to top the berries and garnish with fresh mint. Variation: Add a dollop of cashew cream and garnish with mint.

BERRY
ALMOND
CRISP

· ·

[GF, DF, V]

Bubbling Berry crisps are a hit in any season. This sweet and tangy crisp is easy to modify to be gluten-free without losing any flavor!

ALMOND CRUMBLE TOPPING:

1 cup gluten free rolled oats

½ cup almond meal or gluten free pastry flour

⅓ cup chopped roasted almonds

¼ cup honey or maple syrup

3 tablespoons melted coconut oil

¼ teaspoon ground cinnamon

¼ teaspoon salt

BERRY FILLING:

5-6 cups fresh berries (raspberries, blueberries, strawberries, blackberries)

2 tablespoons cornstarch

1 tablespoon freshly-squeezed lemon juice

1   Preheat oven to 350°F.

2   To make the almond
    crumble topping, stir all
    ingredients together until
    combined, mixing them
    together with your fingers
    if needed. Set aside.

3   Pour the berries into a
    lightly oiled 8 x 8 inch
    baking dish. Sprinkle
    evenly with cornstarch
    and lemon juice (and
    almond extract, if using),
    and toss until evenly
    combined.

4   Sprinkle the almond
    crumble topping evenly
    on top of the berries.

5   Bake for 35-40 minutes,
    or until the topping is
    crisp and golden and the
    fruit is bubbling. Serve
    immediately.

PUMPKIN
SPICE
BARS

· ·

[GF, DF, V]

When you have the pumpkin spice craving, these gluten-free, refined sugar-free bars are the solution!

¾ cup creamy almond butter

½ cup pumpkin puree

1 overripe medium banana

¼ cup maple syrup

1 teaspoon vanilla extract

1 tablespoon coconut flour

1 teaspoon pumpkin pie spice

1 teaspoon cinnamon

1 teaspoon baking soda

¼ teaspoon sea salt

⅓ cup chocolate chips and/or walnuts, optional

1 Preheat oven to 350°F. Lightly oil 8 x 8 inch baking dish with coconut oil.

2 Place almond butter, pumpkin, banana, maple syrup, and vanilla in a medium bowl. Stir well until smooth.

3 Add coconut flour, pumpkin pie spice, cinnamon, baking soda, and sea salt, stirring until smooth.

4 Stir in chocolate chips and walnuts if using.

5 Pour into prepared baking dish, smoothing with a spatula. Bake for 30 minutes or until a knife comes out clean.

EASY VEGAN CHOCOLATE COVERED **STRAWBERRIES**

. . . .

[GF, DF, V]

Who can resist chocolate covered strawberries? They look so fancy, but this romantic dessert only has 2 ingredients!

1 basket of large strawberries, washed, and dried

6-10 ounces of semisweet vegan chocolate chips

1 Line a baking tray with parchment paper.

2 Wash strawberries and pat dry well with a paper towel.

3 In a double boiler over medium heat, melt chocolate, being careful not to introduce any water into the bowl. Stir until smooth.

4 Remove from heat and carefully dip each strawberry, twirling to fully coat each side.

5 Place each coated strawberry on parchment paper and refrigerate to set the chocolate.

CARROT
CAKE

. . . .

[GF, DF, V]

I love a moist carrot cake with warming spices. This healthy carrot cake recipe is one that you can feel good about serving to family and friends.

½ cups milk or unsweetened plant-based milk (almond, cashew, soy, rice)

¾ cup raisins, divided

4 ½ ounces of pitted dates, chopped

½ cup banana, sliced

1 teaspoon pure vanilla extract

1 ¾ cup gluten free rolled oats

2 teaspoons baking powder

2 teaspoons cinnamon

1 teaspoon baking soda

½ teaspoon nutmeg

½ teaspoon ground ginger

⅛ tsp ground cloves

1 ½ cup carrots, finely shredded

½ cup of walnuts, chopped

1   Preheat oven to 350°F. Prepare an 8 x 8 inch pyrex or baking pan by oiling with coconut oil, olive oil, or butter or simply line with parchment paper.

2   In a medium bowl, soak dates, ¼ cup of raisins, banana slices, and vanilla in the milk for 15 minutes to soften dates and raisins.

3   Blend oats in a blender or food processor to form flour. Transfer to a large bowl. Combine with baking powder, cinnamon, baking soda, nutmeg, ginger, and cloves.

4   Add the mixture of milk, soaked dates, bananas, raisins, and vanilla into the blender. Blend until smooth.

5   Combine date mixture and dry ingredients, with a minimum of strokes to make a batter. Add remaining ½ cup of raisins, shredded carrots, and walnuts.

6   Spread batter into prepared baking pan and bake for 40-45 minutes. Cool in pan for 10 minutes before serving.

"CARAMEL" APPLES WITH **PEANUT BUTTER**

. . . .

[GF, DF, V]

These "caramel" apples are made with peanut butter and brown rice syrup, but still look (and taste!) like caramel apples. Very easy to make and sure to please.

6 medium-sized apples (I like Granny Smith or McIntosh)

½ cup creamy, all natural peanut butter, room temperature

½ cup brown rice syrup, room temperature

¾ cup salted and roasted peanuts, chopped

6 wooden sticks

1 Line a tray with parchment paper.

2 Insert a wooden stick into the stem of each apple.

3 In a small pot, combine peanut butter and brown rice syrup over low heat until just heated. Remove from heat. If too stiff, add a small amount of brown rice syrup.

4 With a spatula or spoon, spread the peanut butter and brown rice mixture over the apple and sprinkle with chopped peanuts. Press peanuts lightly to stick. Place apples in refrigerator to chill for 3 hours before serving.

GINGERBREAD

· ·

[GF, DF, V]

The blend of cinnamon, ginger, cloves, allspice, nutmeg, and cloves combine well to create a divine gingerbread.

2 tablespoons of
ground flax seeds
(flax meal)

6 tablespoons
of water

2 cups gluten-free
flour

2/3 cup coconut sugar

3 teaspoons
baking powder

1 teaspoon
baking soda

1/2 teaspoon sea salt

2 teaspoon
ground ginger

1 teaspoon cinnamon

1 teaspoon
ground cloves

½ teaspoon allspice

1/2 cup coconut oil,
melted

1/4 cup blackstrap
molasses

1 cup pumpkin puree

1   Preheat oven to 325 degrees.

2   Grease a 5x 9 (1.5 quart) loaf pan.

3   Prepare your flax eggs by whisking together ground flax seeds and water. Set aside to thicken.

4   In a large bowl, whisk the flour, coconut sugar, baking powder, baking soda, salt, ginger, cinnamon, cloves and allspice together.

5   In a small bowl, mix the melted coconut oil, molasses, pumpkin puree, and flax mixture together.

6   Pour wet ingredients into dry ingredients and mix well to combine.

7   Pour into greased loaf pan.

8   Bake for 50 minutes to 1 hour or until knife comes out clean.

DECADENT RASPBERRY **FUDGE BROWNIES**

. . . .

[GF, DF, V]

Dense, fudgy brownies with raspberries? Yes, please! Frozen raspberries work well in this recipe.

1/3 cup coconut oil, melted

3 large eggs

1/2 cup coconut sugar

1 tsp vanilla extract

1/3 cup unsweetened cocoa powder or raw cacao powder

1/2 cup almond meal or almond flour

¼ teaspoon sea salt

1/2 teaspoon baking soda

1/3 cup chocolate chips (dairy free if vegan)

1 1/2 cups frozen raspberries, roughly chopped

Topping: 1/2 cup frozen raspberries, roughly chopped

1 Preheat oven to 350 degrees.

2 Line a 8 x 8 inch baking pan with parchment paper.

3 In a medium sized bowl mix whisk the eggs, then add coconut oil, coconut sugar, and vanilla. Stir to combine.

4 In a separate bowl combine cocoa powder, almond meal, sea salt and baking soda.

5 Add the dry ingredients to the wet ingredients and stir until combined.

6 Add the chocolate chips and gently stir in 1/2 cup of the frozen raspberries.

7 Pour the batter into the prepared baking tin.

8 Add the remaining 1 cup of chopped frozen raspberries to the top of the batter evenly.

9 Cook for 20-25 min. (20 minutes if your prefer your brownie to be more fudgy, 25 min if you prefer firmer). Brownies should be set around the edges and top, but still fudgy in the middle.

10 Cool for 10 minutes, and then top with the remaining 1/2 cup of frozen raspberries.

11 For easier cutting, and less crumbling, be patient and wait until cooled before cutting and serving.

CARAMEL
DIPPING
SAUCE

. . . .

[GF, DF, V]

This caramel sauce is perfect for dipping fruit or drizzling over your favorite desserts.

Recipe yields about 1 cup

2 Medjool dates, pitted

15.5 ounce can of coconut milk

2 teaspoons cornstarch

¾ cup coconut sugar

1 teaspoon pure vanilla extract

½ teaspoon sea salt

Sliced apples or pears for dipping- optional

1   In a blender, add pitted dates, coconut milk, and cornstarch and blend on high until smooth.

2   In a small pot, add coconut sugar and date mixture and simmer over medium-high heat until sugar is dissolved and mixture appears glossy. Add vanilla extract and salt. Stir to combine.

3   Serve with sliced apples or pears, or drizzle over your favorite dessert.

APRICOT PECAN **BLISS BALLS**

....

[GF, DF, V]

Dried apricots are sweet and tangy. Take these portable treats on the go for a burst of energy, or as a healthy snack to satisfy your sweet craving.

1 cup dried apricots, chopped

½ cup pecans

½ cup gluten free oats

1 teaspoon pure vanilla extract

Shredded coconut-optional

1 In a food processor, pulse apricots. Add pecans and blend on high for 30 seconds. Add oats and vanilla, and pulse until dough forms, about 20 more seconds. You may need to scrape down sides with a spatula.

2 Transfer dough to a bowl and roll to form ½-inch to 1-inch balls.

3 Roll in shredded coconut if desired.

RAW
CHOCOLATE
PUDDING

· ·

[GF, DF, V]

I must admit, the first time I made this recipe my kids were skeptical, but quickly changed their minds when they tasted this smooth, rich, no-cook pudding.

1 cup of peeled, ripe avocado, chopped (1-1½ large avocado)

½ cup unsweetened cocoa powder

1½ teaspoons pure vanilla extract

1 cup of pitted dates, chopped

½ cup freshly-squeezed orange juice

⅛ teaspoon sea salt

1 teaspoon orange zest

1   In a food processor, puree all ingredients together until smooth. You may need to pause and scrape down sides with a spatula a few times while processing.

2   Thin to desired consistency with a teaspoon or two of water or orange juice.

3   Serve in individual cups garnished with orange zest.